THe #1 FUN BooK For DiCe

WoRLd's GReatest DiCe GaMes

compass | labs

Compass Labs • Minneapolis, Minnesota

Editor:	Susan Riley
Project Editor:	Linda Picone
Designer:	Tom Bleakly
Illustrator:	Nancy Hope
Production Artist:	Karin Odell
Copy Editor:	Jacquelyn Fletcher
Production Manager:	Jim Bindas
Operations Manager:	Teri LaFrenz

Table of Contents

More Dice Games

Introduction

Pick up a few dice, shake them, toss them onto a surface—and join the ranks of millions all over the world.

Dice are universal. Once only used for gambling, dice now are part of many family games in the United States. We toss them to determine how many moves to make in board games. We roll them to see who goes first. We cast them to understand statistics. We throw them just to pass the time.

The dice games in this book are for families to play together. Some are complicated; most are not. A few were originally gambling games, but you don't need to use money in order to have fun with them.

So brush up your math skills, get everyone together for a game, and let 'em roll!

The History of Playing Dice

Dice, or something like them, have been around almost as long as people have, and wherever people are.

There were dice games in ancient Egypt, in early China and India, in ancient Greece and Rome, among the American Indians and throughout Medieval Europe. Even during the Stone Age, men used special pebbles to play games with each other.

Dice were probably first used to tell the future. The roll of the dice was thought to be directed by the gods, and the witch-doctor or fortuneteller or wise man could "read" the gods' message in the way the dice landed.

The earliest written records talk about dice, and images of people playing dice can be found in the relics of many ancient cultures. Dice games were part of the cultures in many parts of the world: Africans, Incans, Aztecs, American Indians, Eskimos, Asians...all had—and have—versions of dice. Some were made from small stones, some from fruit pits, some from pottery, some even from animal teeth. Dice made of bone or ivory were common—probably because bone and ivory were easier to make even than stone, so the dice would roll fairly.

Although dice may first have been used to tell the future, dice and "games of chance" have been connected for almost as long. Stories of men rolling the dice to win—or lose—their fortunes, their homes, even their freedom, have been told throughout history. In 99 A.D., the Roman Tacitus described the Germans as playing dice until one man bet his own free-dom. If he lost, he became a slave.

Medieval writers warned Christians of the evils of dice and gambling, but failed to stop the popularity of dice games among both peasants and aristocrats.

But dice could be put to scientific use as well. In the 16th Century, Galileo wrote a paper about probability, using three dice to show why the number 10 would show up more often than the number 9. A century later, the mathematician Blaise Pascal began to explore a question put to him by a gambler, about how often 6s would come up in the roll of one die versus how often double 6s would come up in the roll of two dice. Pascal's work on this problem became the basis of today's probability theory in mathematics.

The opposite faces on a die add up to 7 (1 and 6, 2 and 5, 3 and 4), which may go back to ancient Greece, or even before.

Our culture is filled with images of dice games—from the sight of men hanging around the corner tossing dice onto the sidewalk, to the glitziest casinos in Las Vegas, where men and women in fancy dress roll dice onto a felted tabletop. And, over the years dice have also become part of many family games. When we play dice, we are enjoying a pastime with a long and interesting history.

Dice Hints and Terms

The dice cup

Although you can shake dice in your hand and then roll them, a dice cup makes it easier, especially for smaller hands.

What to put in the pot

Some dice games use chips, pennies or other items to put into a pot. The winner takes the pot at the end. You can buy poker chips, or you can use pennies, but we suggest being creative—and using something other than money—to make sure the games stay fun for everyone. You can use small candies, paper clips, miniature marshmallows, even pretzels.

Who starts

A first toss usually determines who goes first, but you can change that for fun. The youngest person, or the oldest, the person with the first birthday in the year, the person with the most letters in his or her first name are good alternative ways of selecting the first player.

Dice Terminology

There are dozens of dice terms and dice nicknames. Here are just a few that you should be familiar with to play the games in this book.

Cast

A roll of the dice onto a surface.

Counter

Also called a marker, this is used to mark a players place on a board or game card.

Dice

More than one die.

Die

A cube with the numbers 1-6 on its six sides (opposite sides add up to 7).

Face

One side of a die; each die has six faces.

Knucklebones

Pig and sheep knuckles used as one of the earliest forms of dice.

Numbersticks

Four-sided sticks used as a form of dice in the Third Century B.C.

Pips

The spots on a die.

Poker Dice

Special dice with ace, king, queen, jack, 10, and 9 on the faces instead of the numbers 1-6.

Roll

A toss of the dice onto a surface.

Round

One turn for everyone playing the game.

Snake Eyes

Two 1s showing on the dice.

Throw

A roll or toss of the dice, or the total of the faces showing after a roll of the dice.

Toss

A roll of the dice onto a surface.

Let's Play Dice!

⠇⠑⠞⠎⠀⠏⠇⠁⠽

Averages

This game is an easy way to practice basic math.

Object of Averages

To get a score closer to 105 than other players.

Players

2 or more players—more are better

Needed to play

- Three dice
- Paper and pencil

Start

Choose one person to keep score.

Play

Each player throws three dice and tells the sum of the dice to the person keeping score.

At the end of ten rounds, the scores are added.

The person with a score closest to 105 wins. If there is a tie, the three dice are thrown again to break it. The person closest to 105 after that roll wins.

Baseball

Definitely a quieter way to play America's favorite game.

Object of Baseball

To get the most runs in nine innings.

Players

2 players

Needed to play

- One die
- Three counters (or markers) for each player
- Paper (two pieces) and pencil

Start

Draw a baseball diamond on one sheet of paper.

Each player throws the die to decide who is "up to bat." The one with the higher die goes first.

Play

1. Each player's turn is a half-inning. The player is done when three outs are rolled.

2. The bases are all empty at the start of each half-inning.

3. The first player rolls the dice.

4. If a 1, 2, or 3 is rolled, a counter goes on that base.

5. The player rolls again. If another 1, 2, or 3 is rolled, counter moves ahead by the number thrown and another counter goes onto the base of the number shown. For example, if the first throw was a 2, a counter would go on second base. If the second throw is a 1, the counter on second base would move to third base and the new counter would go on first base.

6. Each time a counter comes into home, it counts as a run.

7. A roll of 4 is a home run, and all counters come in to score.

8. A roll of 5 is an out with a counter on base in play.

   If only one counter is on a base when 5 is rolled, that counter is out.

   If there are counters on all the bases, the one on first base is out.

   If there are counters on first and second base, the counter on second base is out.

If there are counters on first and third base, the counter on first base is out.

If there are counters on second and third bases, both are safe—but the roll of the batter is still an out.

9. A roll of 6 is an out, but any counters on bases stay where they are.

10. Three outs end a player's turn, or a half-inning.

11. The other player then rolls until there are three outs.

12. When both players have had their turns, an inning has been played.

13. After nine full innings, the player with the highest score wins.

BasKetbaLL

No dribbling or shooting skills are needed for this very fast game.

Object oF BasKetbaLL

To make the most points in 16 rolls of the dice.

PLayers

2 players, although you can play in teams with more

Needed to pLay

- Two dice
- Paper and pencil

Start

Roll the dice. Player or team with the higher roll starts.

PLay

In a "quarter," each player rolls the dice four times. The total of the dice from those four rolls is the player's score for the quarter.

The player with the highest score after four quarters wins.

Battleship

The hard part is getting the ship, captain and mate—in just that order.

Object of Battleship

To get the most points in ten turns.

Players

3-6

Needed to play

- Dice cup
- Five dice
- Sheet to keep score

Start

Each player rolls the dice. The person who rolls the lowest number starts first.

Play

1. The first player rolls the dice. (Each turn, or round, is three rolls of the dice.)

   If there is not at least one 6 showing, the player rolls all five dice again.

If there is a 6 showing, that becomes the player's "ship." (If more than one 6 shows, only one is counted as the ship.) The player puts the ship aside and throws the other four dice for the second roll.

If there is both a 6 and a 5 showing on the first roll, the player has a ship and a "captain." The player puts those two dice aside and rolls the other three for the second roll.

If there is a 6, a 5, and a 4, the player has a ship, a captain and a "mate." The player puts the 6, 5, and 4 aside and rolls the other two for the second roll.

The ship has to come first, then the captain, then the mate. So if a player throws a 6 and a 4 on the first roll, only the ship counts.

2. Once a player has the ship, captain and mate, it's time to collect a crew.

The lucky player who gets a 6, 5, and 4 on the first roll can take the number showing on the other two dice for the number of crew members.

Or the player can roll the remaining one or both of the dice again, if the numbers showing are low. (The idea is to keep the highest dice.)

The player gets a third roll, if wanted.

If there is a third roll, any dice rolled that time have to be kept, no matter how low.

3. A player gets one point for each crew member.

4. Sometimes a player won't be able to get a ship, captain and mate in the three rolls of the first round. That player gets zero for the round.

5. The dice are passed to the left after a player finishes three rolls.

6. Players who got their ship, captain and mate—and maybe some crew members—keep collecting crew members each round.

7. Each player gets three rolls on a round, and can keep the highest points from each roll, then roll only the remaining dice for the next toss.

8. The player with the most points after everyone has had ten rounds wins.

9. If two players are tied after ten rounds, there is a playoff of one round.

Variation

Instead of using ten rounds to get a winner, the goal can be to see who gets to 100 points first. Each player must get the same number of turns, though, so even if one gets to 100, the others in the game must have their chance to finish. If more than one person has over 100 points, the player with the most points wins.

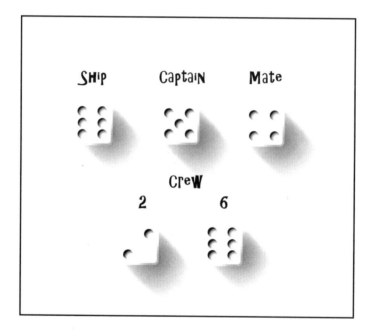

Beetle

This is a dice version of a family game that might seem familiar to you. No plastic parts to keep track of, though, making it easier to play while away from home.

Object of Beetle

To draw a beetle before anyone else.

Needed to play

- One die
- Pencils and paper for each player

Players

Any number can play

Start

Youngest player starts first, then play goes clockwise.

Play

1. Each number of the die stands for one of the beetle's body parts:

   - 1=the body
   - 2=the head
   - 3=each eye (you need two)

- 4=each feeler (you need two)
- 5=each leg (you need six)
- 6=the tail

2. Each player rolls the die once for each turn. A player can draw the body part of the number showing—but only in a certain order:

   - Before you draw any other parts, you must have rolled a 1 so that you can draw the body and add the parts to it.
   - Before you can draw the eyes or feelers, you must have rolled a 2 and added the head to the body.

3. The first to finish drawing a beetle wins.

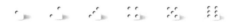

BUNKO

Got a big family? Bunko is the game for you. It's usually played with 12 people.

Object of Bunko

To win the most points yourself, while playing in different teams.

Players

At least 8, more in multiples of 4 (8, 12, 16, etc.)

Needed to play

- A table for every four players
- Three dice for every table
- Score sheet for each player

Start

There are two teams at each table. Partners sit across from each other.

Each player at a table rolls one die; the one with the highest number goes first. Play is clockwise.

Play

1. Each table is ranked. One is the head table, one is the bot-

---

tom table. If there are more than two tables (more than eight people playing), there can be a middle table—or a middle and a middle-plus table.

2. Each player at a table rolls the three dice in turn.

   A 6 counts one point.

   As long as you roll at least one 6 on a turn, you can keep rolling and adding any additional 6s.

   If you roll three 6s, it's a Bunko. You get three points for those 6s.

   But once the three 6s are on the table, everyone at the table rushes to grab a die. Each one collected counts as a point. (If your team rolls a Bunko AND grabs all three dice, it can get six points.)

   If the three dice come up all 1s, it's a "wipeout." A team that rolls a wipeout loses all its points.

3. The head table plays until one of the teams at that table makes 21 points. Then the head table says "stop" (or blows a whistle or rings a cowbell). Play stops at the other tables.

4. The winning scores at other tables can be more than 21, but the play doesn't stop until the winning team at the head table gets 21. (If two teams at a table are tied, play keeps going at that table until one wins a round.) Each player keeps track of the number of times he or she is on a winning team.

5. When a team wins a game, it goes to the next higher table. At the head table, the losers go to the bottom table. Losing teams at the other tables stay where they are.

6. Everyone except the winning team at the head table changes partners after each round. Losers who stay at each table decide which of them will change seats. When the team from the table below sits down, each of them will be paired with one of the losers at that table.

7. The winner at the end of a set number of rounds is the person who has the most wins—in other words, who has been on winning teams the most times. The loser is the person who has the most losses.

Variations

The winner can be the player who rolls the most Bunkos during the game.

CeNteNNiaL

The best first roll in this game is a 1-2-4. Can you figure out why?

Object oF CeNteNNiaL

To be the first player to roll 1 through 12 and then 12 through 1, in order.

PLayers

2 and up—the more the merrier

Needed to pLay

- Three dice
- A pencil and paper for each player

Start

Write the numbers 1 to 12 and then 12 back down to 1 on the paper like this: 1 2 3 4 5 6 7 8 9 10 11 12 12 11 10 9 8 7 6 5 4 3 2 1.

Each player rolls the dice. Highest roll goes first. Play is clockwise.

PLay

You roll the three dice once for each turn.

You have to roll a 1 first. When you roll a 1, you can cross that number off on your sheet.

If you don't roll a 1 on your first roll, you can't cross anything out. The dice go to the next player.

Once you roll a 1, then you have to roll a 2. Then a 3. You can't cross out any number until you've crossed out the number before it.

You can cross out more than one number in a turn.

Here's where it gets complicated: You can use not only the number showing on a die, you can add the dice in a throw. And you can use one die (or all three) more than once. For example: If you throw a 1-2-3 on your first roll, you can cross out 1, 2, and 3. But you can also cross out 4 (1+3), 5 (2+3) and 6 (1+2+3).

When you get to 12, you have to throw one 12 to cross off the 1-12 part of your paper, then another to start back down 12-1. But if you roll three 6s when you're trying to get the first 12, you can scratch off both 12s.

Your turn lasts as long as you keep scoring on each roll.

The first player to cross off all the numbers, going up and down, wins.

Variation

The Matterhorn variation lets players cross off numbers out of order. You have to finish all the 1-12 numbers before starting on the 12-1 numbers, though. In this variation, you only get to roll the dice once each turn, no matter how many numbers you can cross off. You can use the numbers on the dice, or you can add them, but you can only use each die once.

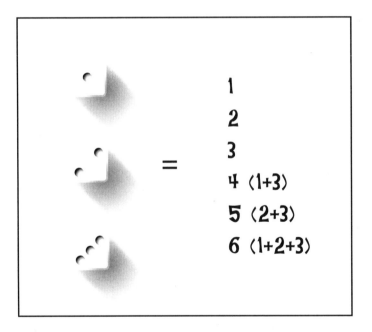

1
2
3
4 (1+3)
5 (2+3)
6 (1+2+3)

CHicago

Object of CHicago

To roll the right number on each turn.

Players

Any number can play

Needed to play

- Two dice
- Pencil and paper

Start

Each player rolls the dice. Highest roll goes first. Play is clockwise.

Play

1. The first player rolls for two points on the first turn. This can be on one or both of the dice.

   If the player rolls a 2, or two 1s, the player gets two points.

   If the player doesn't roll either a 2 or two 1s, the player gets nothing for that round.

2. In each round, the number to roll increases by one. So for the second round, the number players want to roll is three. For the third round it's four, and so on.

3. Players take 11 turns. In the last round, the number to be rolled is 12.

   The person with the most points at the end of 11 rounds wins.

4. If there is a tie at the end of 11 rounds, the tied players roll one die to see who wins.

Variation

To make it a little harder, only allow a number to be counted once in each round. If a player rolled two 5s in the fourth round, for example, only one of them would count.

Cops and Robbers

Object of Cops and Robbers

For a Robber, to get to the hideout of 101 points. For a Cop, to catch one or both of the Robbers.

Players

Four—two Cops and two Robbers

Needed to play

- Four dice, one for each player
- Paper and pencil

Start

All four players roll the dice. The highest score starts.

Play

1. The first player rolls a die and gets that score.

2. The next player will be a Robber (no matter what the first player was); the third player will be a Cop; the fourth player will be whoever is left.

3. Players "move" ahead with the points from each roll of the die.

4. The first Robber starts with 11 points. The second Robber starts with 9.

5. The first Cop starts with three points. The second Cop starts with one point.

6. Although players start in one order, who rolls next changes constantly during play.

   If a player rolls a 6, that player can roll again on the same turn and gets one point if a 1, 2, or 3 is thrown or two points if a 4, 5, or 6 is thrown.

   If a player rolls a 5, the next person to roll is skipped. So if a Robber rolls a 5, the other Robber gets to roll next. If a Cop rolls a 5, the other Cop gets to roll next.

   If a player rolls a 4, the next two people to roll are skipped. If a player rolls the same number as the person before rolled, that player doesn't score in the round.

   If a Cop rolls a 2, the Cop can roll again and count the next roll.

7. Players keep going until all of them have gotten to 101. For a Cop, the goal is to get to 101 before either of the Robbers.

Drop Dead

This game sounds easy, but it's harder than you think to roll five dice without showing a 2 or a 5. The fewer dice you have left, the easier it gets.

Object of Drop Dead

To get the most points by avoiding rolling 2 and 5.

Players

2-6

Needed to play

- Dice cup
- Five dice
- Sheet to keep score

Start

Write each player's name at the top of the sheet so you can keep track of points.

Roll two dice. The player who rolls the highest number starts.

Play

First player rolls five dice.

If no 2 or 5 shows, count the number of points facing up, then roll again.

If there is a 2 or 5 showing, score 0. Take out any 2 or 5—those dice are "dead"—and roll the rest of the dice.

Any time you get a 2 or a 5 on a roll, score 0 for the roll and take out the dice that showed 2 or 5. Then roll the dice you have left.

A turn is as many rolls as it takes to have all the dice go dead. This can be many rolls or only a few—if all of the dice show 2 or 5 on the first roll, they're all dead and the score is 0 for the turn.

When the dice are dead, the first player adds up the points from all of the rolls in that turn.

Dice pass to the next player, who rolls and adds points until all the dice are dead.

Each player takes five turns.

The player with the highest score at the end of five turns wins.

Variation

If you get tired of the numbers 2 and 5, you can pick any opposite sides to be the dead dice. (Remember, opposite sides add up to 7.)

FiFty Up

Easy, but frustrating as you wait for those nasty 3s to show up.

Object oF FiFty Up

To get to 50 points first.

Players

2 players

Needed to play

- Two dice
- Paper and pencil

Start

Each player rolls the dice. Highest roll goes first.

Play

1. The first player throws the dice.

2. The player gets no points unless a double is thrown.

3. A double counts five points, except:
   - Two 3s erase the player's score; you have to start over from zero.

• Two 6s count 25 points.

4. The next player takes a turn.

5. The first person to get 50 points wins.

Variation

Make the goal 100 points, instead of 50.

	=	5 points
	=	5 points
	=	5 points
	=	5 points
	=	25 points
	=	Start Over

Flower Petals

You may not have thought of the dice faces as flowers before, but this game is based on that.

Object of Flower Petals

To have the highest score in four rounds.

Players

Any number can play

Needed to play

- Dice cup
- Three dice
- Score sheet

Start

Each player rolls the dice. The person who rolls the highest number starts. Play is clockwise.

Play

1. The first player rolls the dice three times, counting points on each roll.

   The only dice that count are those that have a central dot. A 1 counts one point. A 3, with two "petals" around the central dot, counts two points. And a 5, with four "petals," counts four points. The 2, 4, and 6 don't count.

But if you roll three 2s, 4s or 6s on a roll—a triplet, your total for the turn is doubled and you get another roll during that turn.

If you roll a second triplet in the same turn, you can't double your score.

2. When each player has had four full turns, the person with the highest score wins.

Variation

You can raise the stakes by starting the game with a pot—of chips, pennies, pretzels, candy, etc. Each player puts in the same number at the beginning of a game; the winner takes the pot. Since the game moves quickly, you may play several games at a sitting, giving everyone a chance to win the pot.

Fruit Machine

A family-friendly version of a slot machine.

Object of Fruit Machine

To win the most markers by the time the other players go bankrupt.

Players

Any number can play

Needed to play

- Three dice
- 100 or more chips, pennies, candies, or game markers
- Four boxes or flat-bottomed bowls of the same size

Start

Each player starts with 5 markers.

Roll one die to determine who starts first.

One box or bowl is filled with 100 or more markers and becomes the bank; the others are left empty.

Play

1. The first player puts one marker in the bank, then rolls a

die into each of the other boxes or bowls.

2. The Fruit Machine bank "pays out" if you roll 6s.

    Two sixes pay out six counters.

    Three sixes pay out 60 counters

3. The player takes winnings from the bank each turn.

4. The game goes on until the players are all bankrupt or the bank goes broke.

Pays 6 counters

Pays 60 counters

Going to Boston

Anyone need a little basic math practice? Try the variation of this game.

Object of Going to Boston

To roll the highest score in a set number of rounds.

Players

3-4 players, but more can play

Needed to play

- Dice cup
- Three dice
- Chips, counters, candies or pennies for each player

Start

Each player rolls two dice. The highest total starts first.

Players decide how many rounds they will play to make a game.

Play

Each player puts a chip or counter into the pot.

A player rolls the three dice.

The die with the highest number showing is left sitting, and the player rolls the other two dice.

Of those two, the die with the higher number is left sitting, and the player rolls the last die a third time.

The total of the three dice after the three rolls is the score for that turn.

When all of the players have rolled the dice three times, the player with the highest score wins that round.

If there's a tie, the players roll another round (or more) until it's broken.

When the agreed number of rounds are finished, the player with the most points wins the pot.

Variation

The play is the same as Going to Boston, but the scoring is different. Dice are thrown in the same way—first all three, then the two lower numbers, then the lower number of the second throw.

The numbers of the first two dice left on the table, after the first and second throw, are multiplied by the number on the third die after the last throw.

HeLp Your NeigHbor

First you want to get rid of your chips—then you want to win so you can get all of them.

Object of HeLp Your NeigHbor

To get rid of your chips first.

PLayers

2-6

Needed to pLay

- Dice cup
- Three dice
- Chips, counters, pennies or candies

Start

1. Each player throws one die.

2. The player with the highest number is the first shooter.

3. The player with the second-highest score is the second shooter. The second shooter sits to the left of the first shooter.

4. Any other players are assigned an order based on the roll of

the die. If they are tied, they roll again to find their place.

5. If there are only two players, the first shooter takes 1, 2 and 3, and the second shooter takes 4, 5 and 6.

6. If there are three players, the first shooter takes 1 and 2, the second shooter takes 3 and 4, and the third shooter takes 5 and 6.

7. If there are four players, they each take a number, 1, 2, 3 or 4, in order. Numbers 5 and 6 are dead.

8. If there are five players, number 6 is dead.

Play

The players start with ten chips each.

The first shooter throws the dice. Any player whose number—or numbers—comes up has to put a chip in the pot for each one.

The dice pass to the second shooter, for the same kind of play.

The first player without any chips wins—and collects the pot.

The second shooter starts the next game—and takes the numbers of the first shooter from the first game.

For example, in a game with three people, the second shooter would have 3 and 4 in the first game. That player would start the second game, and would have the numbers 1 and 2 for that game.

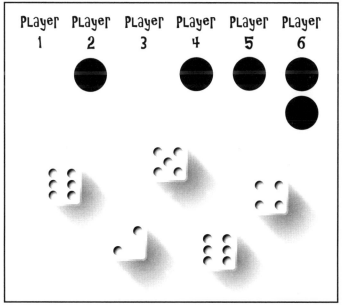

On a roll of 2,4,5,6,6

Player 1 receives 0 chips   Player 4 receives 1 chip
Player 2 receives 1 chip   Player 5 receives 1 chip
Player 3 receives 0 chips   Player 6 receives 2 chips

Hooligan

A simpler version of a popular commercial game.

Object of Hooligan

To roll multiples of each dice face, one turn at a time.

Players

Any number can play

Needed to play

- Dice cup
- Five dice
- Paper and pencil

Start

Each player rolls the dice. Highest score starts. Play is clockwise.

Make a score sheet with seven sections: 1, 2, 3, 4, 5, 6 and Hooligan, with the name of each player across the top.

Play

1. Each player gets three throws in a turn. After the first roll of a turn, the player can say which of the sections on the score sheet the player is trying for. Any dice with that num-

ber are put aside, and the player rolls the remaining dice again.

After the second roll, if more of the dice show the number the player is trying for, those, too, can be put aside and the player can roll whatever dice are left.

If none of the desired number show, the player can roll all of the remaining dice again.

2. A player can decide to roll all of the dice again after a first roll, if none of the numbers showing are useful, and then decide what section to choose after the second roll. There still is only one more roll for that player on that turn.

3. At the end of the three rolls, the player adds the number of dice showing the desired number and multiplies by the number itself.

   Example: The player is trying to finish the 4 section on the score sheet. The first roll shows 1-1-2-3-4. The player puts aside the 4 and rolls the remaining dice. The second roll is 2-4-4-6. The player puts aside the two 3s and rolls the remaining two dice, which show 2-5. The total number of 4s for the turn is 3, so the player multiplies 4 by 3, for a score of 12 in the 4 section.

4. If a player rolls all five dice to the number wanted on the

first or second throw, the maximum is scored and the player can roll all of the dice for the next throw, again putting aside any that show the desired number—and counting those extra points in that section of the score sheet.

5. Players can try to roll points for each section of the score sheet on only one turn. They have to pick a different section for each of their turns.

6. A Hooligan is a straight of either 1-2-3-4-5 or 2-3-4-5-6. It counts 20 points. A player can shoot for a Hooligan any time during the game. If the player has filled all other parts of the score sheet in six turns, the player must make a Hooligan on the last turn or score zero in that part of the score sheet.

7. The player with the most points at the end of seven rounds wins.

INdiaN Dice

Object of Indian Dice

To make the highest poker hand.

Players

Any number can play

Needed to play

- Dice cup
- Five dice
- Chips, pennies or candies

Start

Each player rolls two dice. Highest score starts. Play is clock-wise.

Play

1. Each player puts a chip into the pot.

    The player who rolls first can have up to three throws to make a "hand."

2. After the first roll, the player can stand, or can pick up any or all of the dice and roll them again.

---

3. After the second roll, again the player can stand, or can roll any or all of the dice again.

   The hands are ranked in this order:
   - Five of a kind
   - Four of a kind
   - Full house (three of one kind, two of another)
   - Three of a kind
   - Two pairs
   - Pair
   - No pair

   The value of similar hands is based on the numbers that make it up (three 6s rank higher than three 4s, for example)

4. The next players can take only the same number of rolls on their turns as the first player did.

   Example: If the first player decided to stand after the first roll, the other players can only have one roll in the first round.

5. The person winning the round gets the pot.

6. The player to the left of the first player starts the second round.

---

7. A game usually is just two rounds, or three if there are only two players, but you can decide how many you want to play.

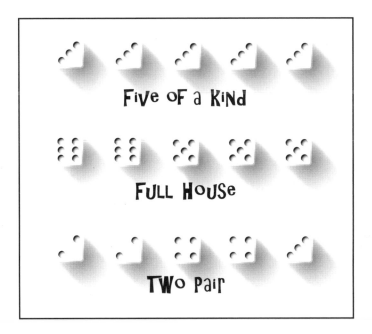

Jackpot

You can use candy, cookies, pretzels or other goodies instead of chips. Just don't eat them before the game is over.

Object of Jackpot

To win the most chips.

Players

Any number can play

Needed to play

- Two dice
- Poker chips
- A big sheet of paper (more than 12 inches each direction)

Start

1. Draw a big circle in the middle of the paper, at least 12 inches across.

2. Divide the circle into nine equal pie-shaped pieces. Number the pieces 3 through 11.

3. Give an equal number of poker chips (or pennies or even candies) to each player.

4. Each player rolls the dice. The one who rolls the highest number starts. Play is clockwise.

Play

The first player throws the dice, then adds up the numbers on the two. The player puts a chip on the slice of the circle with the number thrown. If you throw a 2 and a 3, you would put a chip on the 5 circle.

The second player rolls, adds, then puts a chip on a slice of the circle.

As soon as a slice has three chips on it, the next player to roll that number wins those chips.

A player who rolls snake-eyes—two 1s—has to put a chip on every slice that doesn't already have three chips on it.

A player who rolls a 12 gets to take all the chips on the circle.

You can keep playing for as long as you want, or until one person has all of the chips.

If one player drops out (because all of his or her chips are gone), everyone else can keep playing if they want.

Le Drinquet

Careful rolling is the trick in this game.

Object of Le Drinquet

To get 101 points by rolling the dice on your color.

Players

Two can play

Needed to play

- A checkerboard or chessboard
- Three dice
- Paper and pencil

Start

Players decide who is Black and who is White (or Red).

Each player rolls the dice. Highest roll goes first.

Play

The first player rolls the dice onto the board.

Dice that land entirely inside squares of the person's color can be counted. Dice that land on squares of the other color, or that have any part of them lying in squares of the other color, don't count.

The player adds the number of points on any dice completely within the squares of the right color.

Players take turns until one person gets to 101 points.

Variations

The game can be played with one or two dice, instead of three.

7 points

Liar's Dice

If you've got some budding actors and actresses in your family, this game can be wild.

Object of Liar's Dice

To fool the other players—and to be the best guesser yourself.

Players

Three or more

Needed to play

- Dice cup
- Five dice
- Three chips, counters, candies or pennies for each player

Start

Each player rolls one die. Highest number starts. Play is clockwise.

Play

1. The first player rolls the dice, but keeps them covered after the roll so the other players can't see them.

2. The player then tells the others what has been rolled:
   - Five of a kind

- Four of a kind
- Straight=the numbers are in order, 1-2-3-4-5
- Full house=three of one number, two of another
- Three of a kind

3. In describing the roll, the player gives details, such as "full house, 5s on 2s" (three 5s, two 2s).

4. The player can tell the truth about the dice—or can lie.

5. Once the first player has described the roll—whether it's true or not—the player to the left can decide to accept the description or to challenge it.

6. If the next player accepts the throw, that player takes over the dice—still keeping them hidden from other players.

   The second player can roll none, some, or all of the dice, but must tell the other players how many, if any, have been rolled.

   The second player now describes the dice. That description can be accepted or challenged by the next player.

7. If the second player challenges the first player's description, the dice are revealed. If the first player lied, the first player puts a chip in the pot. If the first player told the truth, the challenger pays into the pot.

8. After a challenge, no matter who won, the second player takes the dice and rolls a new turn.

9. A player is out after losing all three chips.

10. The last person with chips wins—and collects the pot.

Four of a Kind?

Long-Distance Doubles

This is very simple, but you can make it last a long time. It's a good way to pass time when waiting in a doctor's office or on a car trip.

Object of Long-Distance Doubles

To roll the highest number in 180 turns.

Players

2 people can play

Needed to Play

- One die
- Paper and pencil

Start

Each player rolls the die. The person with the highest number starts.

Put five columns on the paper, numbered from 0 to 5.

Play

1. Each of you rolls the die on a turn.

2. The person with the higher number subtracts the lower

number and marks the difference as the score for that turn.

For example, if you roll a 6 and the other player rolls a 2, you score 4 for the turn.

If you both roll the same number, the score is zero.

3. The winner is the player with the highest total after 180 turns.

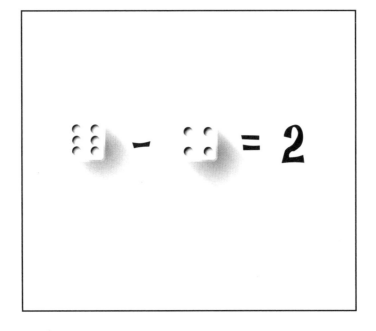

Odds Against Evens

Object of Odds Against Evens

To get the most points by rolling either odd or even numbers.

Players

Two can play

Needed to play

- Three dice
- Paper and pencil

Start

Each player rolls one die. The person with the higher number starts.

Play

1. The starting player can choose Evens (2, 4, 6 or a total of 12) or Odds (1, 3, 5 or a total of 9).

2. The other player gets whichever is left, Odds or Evens.

3. The starting player rolls the three dice. The only dice that count for that player are those with that player's values.

---

4. A player scores the face value of the dice that count. For example, if the first player chose Evens and rolls a 1-2-6, the 2 and 6 count. The player gets 8 points for that turn.

5. The person with the highest score after 20 rounds wins.

Variation

Players can change Odds and Evens after ten rounds.

Pass 10

Object of Pass 10

To win the pot by rolling 11s and 12s.

Players

Two or more; a good game for a large group

Needed to play

- Dice cup
- Two dice
- A lot of counters, pennies, candies or other markers

Start

Divide the counters among the players.

Roll the dice. Whoever has the highest combination starts. Play is clockwise.

Play

1. The first player puts two counters into the pot. If an 11 or 12 is rolled, the player gets the pot. If not, the counters stay in the pot and the dice go to the next person.

2. Each following player puts two counters in the pot, then

rolls the dice. If an 11 or 12 is rolled, that player gets the pot.

3. After a win, the next player starts the pot all over again. You drop out when all of your counters are gone. The last player to collect the pot wins. Or the person with the most counters after "time" is called.

WiNS tHe pot!

Pig

Object of Pig

To reach 100 points.

Players

Any number can play

Needed to play

- Dice cup
- Score sheet
- Two dice

Start

Each player rolls the dice. The person with the highest score starts. Play is clockwise.

Play

1. The first player rolls the dice. If the player rolls a 1, the score is zero and the dice go to the next player.

2. If no 1 shows, the player scores the number of points on the dice and can either pass the dice or roll again.

3. You roll as many times as you want and keep adding up

the points—unless you roll a 1. If you do, you lose all the points you made on that turn.

4. If you roll doubles (of anything but 1) you can double your score for that roll. So if you roll two 6s, you score 24 on that roll.

5. If you roll two 1s, you score 25 on that roll.

6. The first player to get to 100 points wins, but every player must get the same number of turns.

Variation

You can play with just one die.

PyraMid Dice

This game moves fast as you go up the pyramid—mainly because someone loses as the number of dice gets smaller.

Object of PyraMid Dice

To get to the top of the pyramid without rolling the "wrong" number.

PLayers

Two can play

Needed to pLay

- Five dice
- Paper and pencil

Start

1. Draw a pyramid with five squares at the base, then four squares on top of that, three squares on top of that, two squares, then one.

2. Number the squares in each row. On the bottom row, the squares will be 1-2-3-4-5. On the next row they will be 1-2-3-4, and so on until the square at the top is numbered 1.

3. Roll one die to decide who starts.

Play

The first player rolls the dice. The player can fill in one of the squares on the bottom row using one of the numbers from the first throw. (For example, if the roll is 2-3-3-4-6, the player can chose to fill in the 2, 3, or 4 square.) If a player rolls all 6s, that turn is lost.

The second player does the same thing. Each box can only be filled once.

On the second turn, the first player rolls just four dice.

The player can fill in one of the squares on the next row from the bottom, using one of the numbers from the roll. If the player rolls only 5s and 6s, the turn is lost.

The second player does the same.

For the third turn, three dice are used. If the player rolls only 4s, 5s and 6s, the turn is lost.

For the fourth turn, two dice are used. The player loses the turn if no 1 or 2 is thrown.

For the fifth turn, one die is used. A 1 must be thrown.

Players keep moving to the top of the pyramid until one loses by being unable to fill a square.

Sequences

Object of Sequences

To reach 100 points.

Players

Any number can play

Needed to play

- Dice cup
- Six dice
- Score sheet

Start

Each player rolls the dice; highest score starts. Play is clockwise.

Play

1. Each player rolls the six dice once on a turn.

2. You can score points on your turn only if the six dice have one or more of these sequences:
   - 1-2   5 points
   - 1-2-3   10 points
   - 1-2-3-4   15 points

- 1-2-3-4-5   20 points
- 1-2-3-4-5-6   25 points
- Five 6s   30 points
- Six 6s   60 points

If you don't have at least a 1-2 in a roll, you don't score any points on that turn.

Each die can be used in only one sequence. For example, if you roll a 1-2-2-3-3-4, you can only count the 1-2-3-4 sequence for 15 points. The 1 can't be used to make any more sequences.

You can count two sequences in a turn, if you have the right dice. For example, if you roll 1-1-2-2-3-3, you have two sequences of 1-2-3, each one counting 10 points.

If you have four or more 1s on a roll, you lose all the points you've won so far. You have to start over from zero.

3. After you've rolled the dice for your turn, you add up your points for the turn and pass the dice to the next player.

4. When one players gets 100 points, the rest of the players finish their turns for that inning, and the game is over.

5. The person with the highest score wins.

Variation

You can make it easier to score—and a faster game—by changing the scoring slightly. In this variation, the scoring is:

- 1   5 points
- 1-2   10 points
- 1-2-3   15 points
- 1-2-3-4   20 points
- 1-2-3-4-5   25 points
- 1-2-3-4-5-6   30 points
- Five 6s   35 points
- Six 6s   70 points

The other rules are the same.

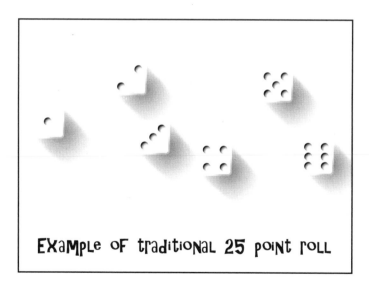

EXaMPLe oF traditioNaL 25 poiNt roLL

Shut the Box

A little strategy is needed—as well as luck.

Object of Shut the Box

To cover as many boxes as possible.

Players

Two or more

Needed to play

- Two dice
- Nine chips or counters
- Sheet of paper with nine boxes on it, numbered 1-9

Start

Each player rolls the dice. Highest score starts. Play is clockwise.

Play

1. The first player rolls the dice and totals the number showing.

2. The player tries to cover two boxes on the sheet, using the total of the dice.

Example: If the player rolled a 5 and a 4, the total for the roll is 9. The player can cover the 1 and 8, 2 and 7, 3 and 6, or 4 and 5 boxes.

3. The first player rolls again, and tries to cover two more boxes. This time, the player can't make a combination using any number already covered.

   Example: If the player covered the 2 and 7 on the first roll, then rolls a 3 and 4 on the second roll, the player can cover any two boxes that add up to 7—but not the 2 and 5, because the 2 has already been covered.

4. After the 7, 8 and 9 boxes have been covered, the player only uses one die, not two. But two boxes still must be covered after each roll.

5. When a player can't cover two boxes, that player's turn is over. The boxes left uncovered are added. That total is the player's penalty score.

6. The player with the lowest penalty score after everyone has had a turn, wins.

Sing Luk

The name is similar to "four, five, six" in Chinese.

Object of Sing Luk

To win the other players' counters.

Players

At least four players are needed

Needed to play

- Dice cup
- Three dice
- Chips, pennies, counters or play money for each player

Start

Each player rolls the dice. The person with the highest roll starts first.

Each player puts in the same number of chips, pennies, etc., for a stake.

Play

1. The first player throws until one of these combinations shows:
   - Three of a kind, or *wai*

- 4-5-6, or *sing luk*
- Two of a kind
- 1-2-3, or *mo lung*

2. If the first player rolls *wai, sing luk* or two of a kind with the third die a 6, he or she wins the stake from the other players.

3. The player passes the dice clockwise if the throw shows two of a kind, with the third die a 5, 4, 3 or 2.

4. The player loses the total of the other players' stakes if a *mo lung* is rolled, or two of a kind, with the odd die a 1.

5. The game goes on until one player has won all of the stakes, or for a set time limit.

TWenty-One

Luck plays an even bigger role in this game than it does in the well-known gambling table version.

Object of Twenty-One

To get close—but not over—21 points each turn.

Players

Any number, but 4-6 is best

Needed to Play

- Dice cup
- Five dice
- Paper and pencil
- Chips, pennies, candies or game markers

Start

Each player gets the same number of chips or markers.

Each player puts the same number of chips or markers in the kitty.

Each player rolls the dice. Highest roll goes first. Play is clockwise.

Play

1. The first player rolls four of the dice and tries to get a total of 21.

   If the roll is 21, the player wins the whole kitty.

   If the score is more than 21, the player loses the round.

   If the score is less than 21, the player can "stick" or can roll the remaining die to try to get closer to 21. Whatever shows on that roll is added to the sum of the first four dice. If the number now is more than 21, the player loses the round. If it's less than 21, the player can stick or can roll the die again.

2. When a player decides to stick—or goes over 21—it's the next player's turn.

3. The person who scores closest to 21 in a round wins the kitty. If two or more people get the same score, they share the kitty.

Yacht

This is a do-it-yourself version of a popular family game.

Object of Yacht

To roll certain combinations of dice in 12 turns.

Players

Any number can play

Needed to play

- Five dice
- Score sheets

Start

Set up the score sheets this way:
- Yacht (five of a kind)=50
- Big Straight (2-3-4-5-6)=30
- Little Straight (1-2-3-4-5)=30
- Full House (three of one number, two of another)=total of the dice thrown
- Choice (any five dice)=total of the dice thrown
- 1s=total sum of 1s thrown during one turn
- 2s=total sum of 2s thrown during one turn
- 3s=total sum of 3s thrown during one turn
- 4s=total sum of 4s thrown during one turn

- 5s=total sum of 5s thrown during one turn
- 6s=total sum of 6s thrown during one turn

Each player rolls two dice. The person who rolls the highest number starts. Play is clockwise.

Play

1. Each player gets 12 turns. On each turn, you can pick up and roll again as many of the dice as you want on the second and third roll, to try to make the combination you need.

2. For each turn you must cross off and score one of the 12 categories. You can pick a category even if you don't have what you need, and score it zero. For example, if you are trying to roll a Little Straight, and end up with a 1-3-3-4-5, you can count it for your 3s (which would be 6 points), for your Choice (which would be 16), for your 1s (which would be 1), etc.

3. At the end of 12 turns, the player with the highest score wins.

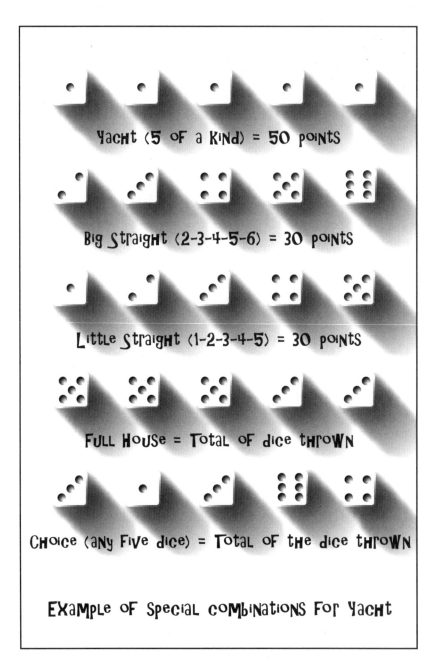

Yacht (5 of a Kind) = 50 points

Big Straight (2-3-4-5-6) = 30 points

Little Straight (1-2-3-4-5) = 30 points

Full House = Total of dice thrown

Choice (any Five dice) = Total of the dice thrown

Example of Special combinations For Yacht